LIGHT
AND LASERS

Design   Cooper · West

Editor   Margaret Fagan

Researcher   Cecilia Weston-Baker

Illustrator   Louise Nevett

Consultant   J. W. Warren Ph.D.
                Formerly Reader in Physics
                Education, Department of
                Physics, Brunel University,
                London, U.K.

J535
W44

1. Light
2. Lasers

Designed and produced by
Aladdin Books Ltd
70 Old Compton Street
London W1

*First published in the
United States in 1986 by*
Gloucester Press
387 Park Avenue South
New York NY 10016

ISBN 0-531-17033-0

Printed in Belgium

Library of Congress Catalog
Card Number: 86-80626

87-03115

SCIENCE TODAY

LIGHT
AND LASERS

Kathryn Whyman

GLOUCESTER PRESS
New York·Toronto·1986

INTRODUCTION

Our sense of sight is one of our most important links with the world. We can see thousands of colors and shapes which help us to recognize the people, places and things around us. But our eyes are limited. Not until the discovery of lenses were we able to see the things that were either too small or too far away for our eyes to focus on.

Lenses in microscopes allow us to see tiny forms of life, helping us to understand how living things function. And lenses in telescopes have enabled us to understand something of the solar system, and the universe, of which we are a tiny part. In this book you will read more about light and lenses. And you will learn how a special type of light, laser light, is changing our lives.

CONTENTS

LIGHT AND DARKNESS

Our most important source of light is the Sun. But where does sunlight come from? The Sun has an enormous amount of energy that is given out in the form of heat – at its center, the temperature of the Sun is about 23 million degrees Fahrenheit! It is some of this energy that reaches us as light.

Since the Earth spins around once every 24 hours, we only face the Sun part of the time – the time we call "day." At night, light from the Sun can no longer reach us. But even at night there is some light. The stars, like the Sun, produce light. The Moon also provides light. But the Moon has no light of its own – it simply reflects light that has reached it from the Sun.

Electric lights enable aircraft to land safely at night

At night, we see how the Moon reflects the Sun's light

HOW DOES LIGHT TRAVEL?

Light travels very fast indeed – faster than anything else we know of. The Sun is about 93 million miles away from Earth and yet its light takes only about eight minutes to reach us! Some of the stars are so far away that their light takes many years to reach us. We do not see them as they are, but as they were hundreds, thousands, or even millions of years ago!

Sometimes you can see rays of light from the Sun as they light up clouds and dust particles in the air. You can see that the rays do not bend or curve – they seem to travel in straight lines. Light from a spotlight travels in the same way. Its beam has straight edges. If rays of light changed direction as they traveled through the air, you would be able to see around corners!

Light travels in straight lines
Light from the flashlight travels through the holes in the first screen. But only the rays traveling through the center hole have a straight path through all three screens.

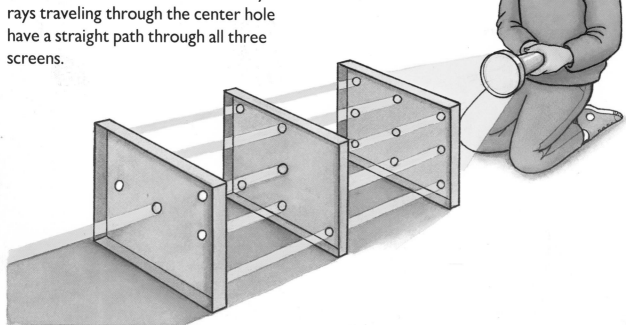

9

Performers in the spotlight

MAKING SHADOWS

Light can travel through some materials; it can pass through air, water and glass. Materials that allow light to pass through them are "transparent." Some materials allow a little light to travel through them, but others are "opaque." Wood, metal and bricks are opaque. They do not let light through them. When light shines onto an opaque object, a shadow is formed.

You can make shadows yourself by shining a light onto the wall of a dark room. An opaque object, such as a pen, placed between the light and the wall, will cast a shadow on the wall. On a bright sunny day, you can see clear shadows outside. Shadows fall wherever the light of the Sun is blocked by trees, hedges, buildings or any other opaque object. Because your own body is opaque, it will cast shadows onto the ground.

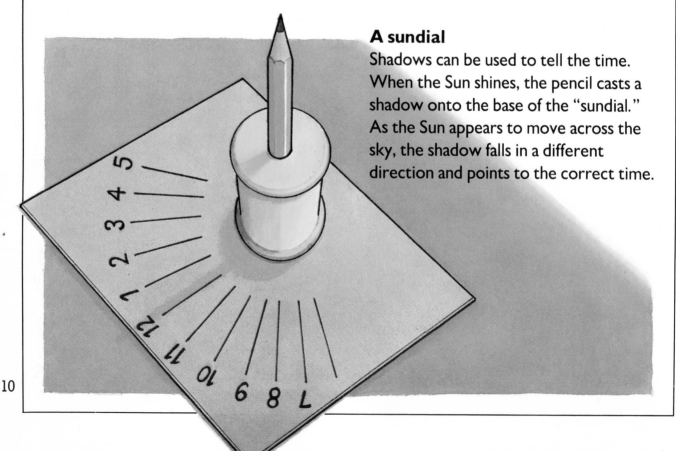

A sundial
Shadows can be used to tell the time. When the Sun shines, the pencil casts a shadow onto the base of the "sundial." As the Sun appears to move across the sky, the shadow falls in a different direction and points to the correct time.

THE ECLIPSE OF THE SUN

Sometimes the Moon passes between the Sun and the Earth in such a way that all three are in a straight line. The Moon is opaque and so it casts a shadow onto the surface of the Earth. The part of the Earth in the shadow is suddenly thrown into darkness in the daytime! If you are standing in a shadowed area looking at the Sun, you may only be able to see part of it (called a "partial" eclipse) or it may be obscured altogether by the Moon – a "total" eclipse. **The light of the Sun can be blinding. You must never look directly at the Sun.**

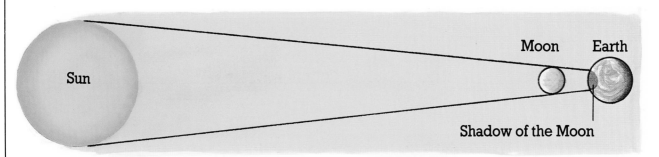

A partial eclipse of the Sun: the Moon passes over part of the Sun

REFLECTIONS

We know that light shines onto every object we see. But this light does not just disappear – some of it bounces off the object again. We say it is "reflected." We can only see objects when they reflect light. Our houses, roads, trees and flowers have no light source of their own. We see them because they reflect the Sun's light.

Every substance reflects some light. Shiny, smooth surfaces, such as metals, are the best reflectors of light. A mirror, made from a sheet of glass with a thin layer of silver or aluminum on the back, reflects light almost perfectly. However, a mirror image can be misleading. You appear the wrong way around in an ordinary mirror – left appears right and vice versa, and your reflection may be very distorted in a curved mirror.

Mirror images

Letters held in front of a mirror appear the wrong way around in the reflection. We say they are "laterally inverted." But if a second mirror is added, at right angles to the first, the image is turned around again.

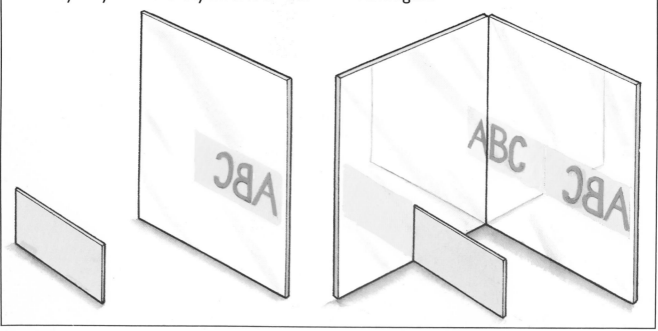

The glass walls of this building reflect a mirror image of the street

REFRACTION

When light travels from one transparent material to another, it changes direction. Light bends as it travels from air into glass or water. It bends again as it leaves glass or water and reenters the air. We call this bending of light "refraction." But why should light bend like this? The reason is that light travels more slowly in glass or water than it does in air: light travels more slowly through dense materials. If a ray of light enters water at an angle, it changes direction as it is slowed down.

Refraction of light has some strange effects. It can make a stick look bent when it is lowered into water; it makes the bottom of a swimming pool seem closer than it really is; it can even make a traveler "see" lakes in the desert, as in a mirage.

When you look at a spoon in a glass of water, you see the light that the spoon reflects. Light from the spoon handle travels to your eyes in a straight line. But light from the rest of the spoon changes speed and direction as it passes from water to air. However, your brain assumes that the light reaching your eyes has all traveled in straight lines. You see a bent spoon which seems closer to you than it is.

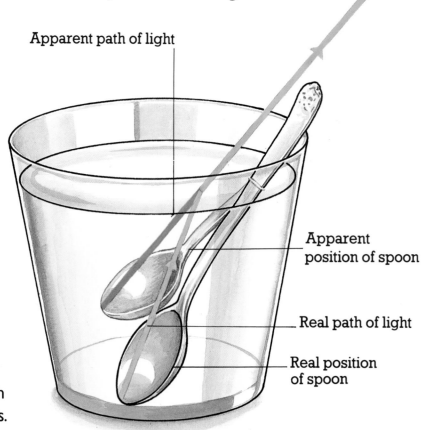

Apparent path of light

Apparent position of spoon

Real path of light

Real position of spoon

14

Mirages are caused by light bending as it passes through warm air

Light from this flashlight is traveling from cool air to the warmer air above the candle. Warm air is less dense than cold air, so light travels faster in it and bends, or is refracted. A distorted image can be seen on the screen. This same shimmering effect is produced on a hot day. Light travels faster through the hot air rising from the ground than through the cooler air above.

SPLITTING LIGHT

A ray of light from the Sun, or from an electric light bulb, looks white. But this white light is really a mixture of lights of different colors! To see these colors, we must split up the white light by shining it through a glass "prism." White light is refracted as it enters and leaves the prism. Each of the different colors of light travels at a slightly different speed through the glass. As they leave the prism, they each bend by a different amount. The main colors – red, orange, yellow, green, blue, and violet – can be seen clearly. They are called the "spectrum." We can see the colors of the spectrum naturally in soap bubbles, thin films of oil or rainbows.

You can make white light by mixing light of different colors together. This spinning wheel is divided into equal sections. Each section is painted with a different color from the spectrum. As the wheel spins, the colors "mix" together and the wheel looks white!

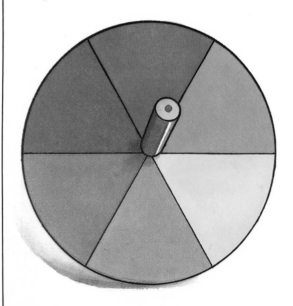

White sunlight may be split into the colors of the spectrum by raindrops. White light bends as it enters the edge of the drop of water. It is then reflected back into the drop and is bent once more as it leaves the drop. The colors of the spectrum are now spread out. Thousands of raindrops together may separate sunlight in this way and form a rainbow, one of the most beautiful natural sights of all.

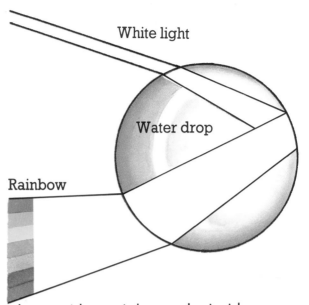

White light

Water drop

Rainbow

The colors of the rainbow range from red on the outside to violet on the inside

MIXING COLORED LIGHT

As you look at this page, you are seeing the light it is reflecting. It is probably reflecting sunlight or electric light, both of which are "white." Yet you can see many different colors on the page. To understand how we see colors, you have to remember that white light is really a mixture of colors. The white part of the page is reflecting all the colors of the spectrum together. But the printed words are reflecting almost no light. Black is the absence of color, or light. The other parts of the page are reflecting some parts of the spectrum but not others. The colors we see depend on the type of light being reflected.

Three of the colors of the spectrum – red, green and blue – are known as the primary light colors. It is possible to make *any* color just by mixing different amounts of these three colors.

Here you can see some of the effects of mixing the primary colors of light. Red and green together make yellow light; green and blue combine to make cyan; and blue and red give magenta. Any other color can be produced by varying the amounts of each of the primary colors. Red, blue and green together make white.

Magenta

Cyan

MIXING COLORED PAINT

Red, blue and yellow are said to be the primary colors of paint. Blue paint reflects green light as well as blue. Yellow paint reflects green and red light. A mixture of blue and yellow paint appears green since this is the only color reflected by both. An artist can mix paints to produce any color.

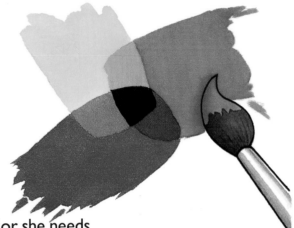

An artist mixes paint to make the shade of color she needs

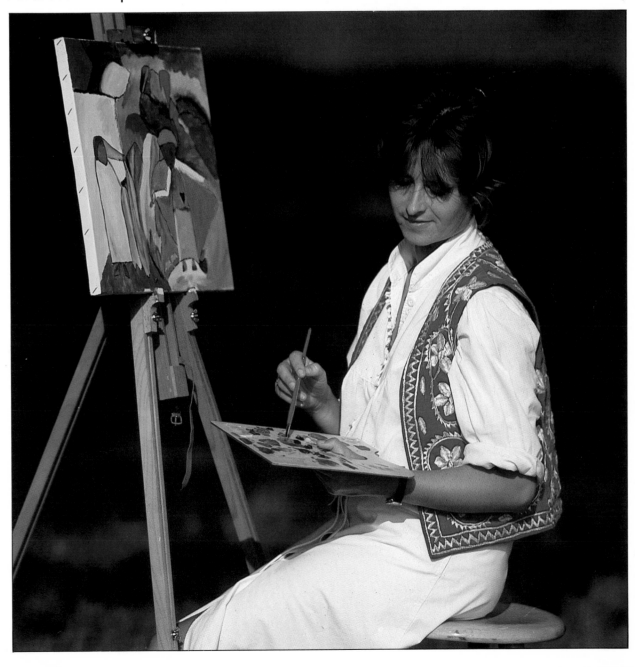

LENSES

Lenses are pieces of transparent material, such as glass or plastic, which have been made into special shapes. They refract (bend) light in certain ways depending on their shape. Lenses may be convex or concave. Convex lenses are thicker in the middle than they are at the edges. Concave lenses are thinnest in the middle.

A convex lens

Light rays from a small, close object travel in straight lines to the lens. But as they pass through the lens and toward your eye, they bend inward. Since your brain expects light to travel in straight lines, you see a larger (magnified) image.

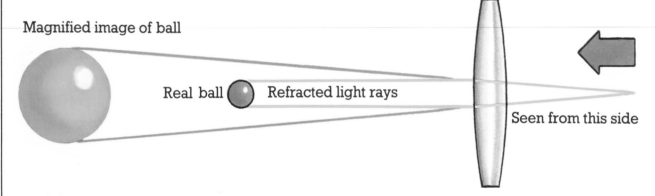

Magnified image of ball

Real ball Refracted light rays

Seen from this side

A concave lens

Rays of light from a tennis ball travel in straight lines to the lens. As they pass through the lens, they bend outward toward your eyes. Again, the brain expects these rays to have arrived in straight lines and you see a smaller image.

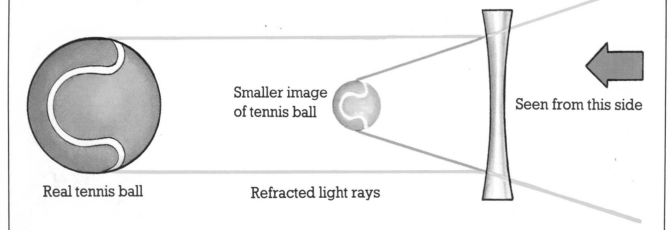

Smaller image of tennis ball

Seen from this side

Real tennis ball Refracted light rays

Convex and concave lenses are very useful. They are found in many of the instruments that help us to see things that we could not see with our eyes alone. Lenses are used in telescopes, which help us see stars and planets; in binoculars, which enable us to watch birds and animals in the wild; and in microscopes, which magnify tiny living things.

Scientists use microscopes to carry out detailed work

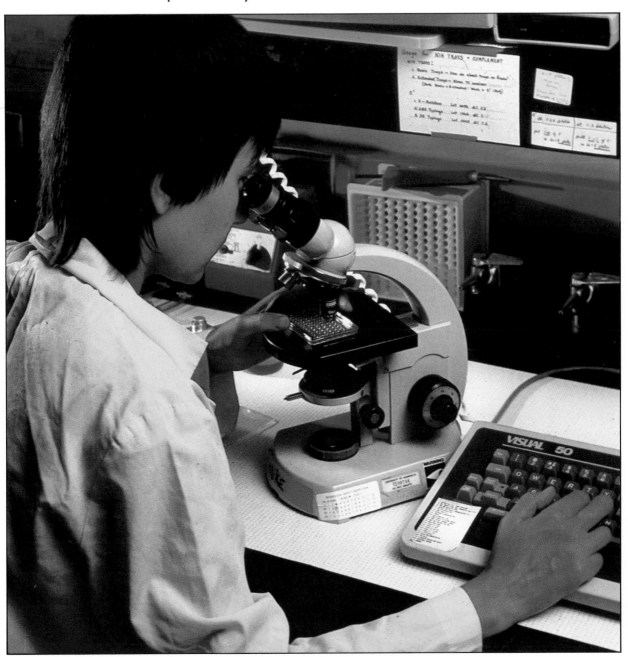

HOW WE SEE

It is light that enables our eyes to see. Light reflected from this page enters each eye and passes through a hole called the "pupil." In dim surroundings, your pupils get larger to let in more light and in bright light, they become smaller. Your eyes each contain a lens. This lens is jelly-like and can change shape. The lens bends the light entering your eyes so that you always see a clear picture. At the back of the eye is a "screen" called the "retina." When light rays fall onto the retina, they cause messages to be sent to the brain. These messages are sent along nerve fibers. Your brain interprets the messages it receives and you are conscious of "seeing."

An optician may suggest you wear glasses or contact lenses to improve poor eyesight.

Opticians use different lenses to check a patient's eyesight

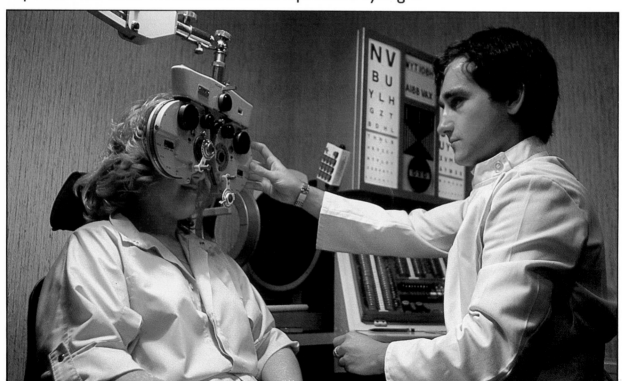

The pinhole camera

This simple camera is a box with a pinhole at the front. Rays of light from the candle travel in straight lines through the pinhole to the screen at the back. The rays cross over as they pass through the hole and so the image is formed upside down.

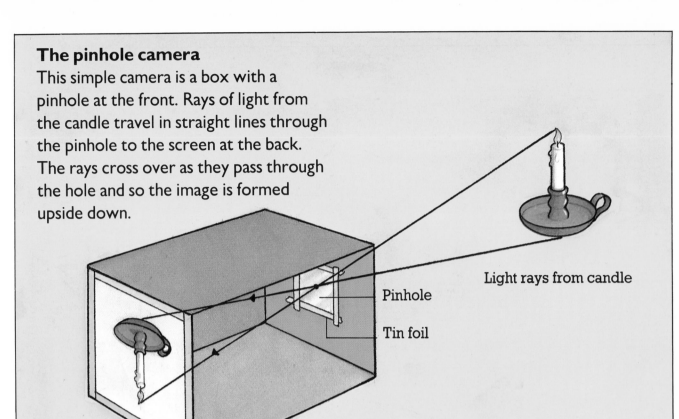

Light rays from candle

Pinhole

Tin foil

Tracing paper

Box that shuts out light

The eye works a little like the pinhole camera. An apple held in your hand reflects rays of light that pass through your eye. The lens becomes short and fat to focus the light rays onto your retina. To focus on the apple tree, which is further away, your lens gets longer and thinner. The image formed on your retina is upside down in both cases. But when the information is relayed from your retina to your brain, you "see" things the right way up.

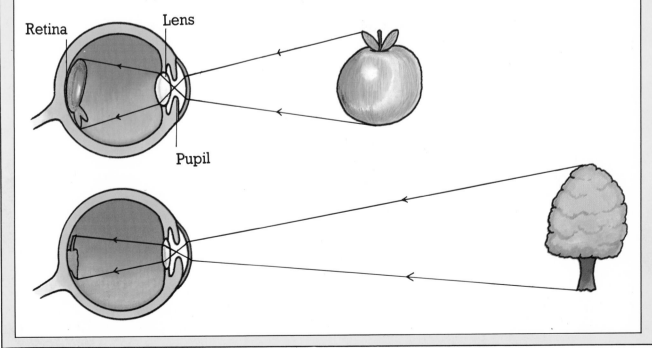

Retina

Lens

Pupil

23

LASERS

Lasers produce a very special sort of light. We have seen that white light is a mixture of many colors which can be separated. It helps to think of these colors as waves – rather like the waves you can make by shaking a rope up and down. Each different color of light has a different length of wave. Red light has long waves whereas blue light has short waves. The light produced by a laser is all of the same wavelength.

This means that a beam of light produced by a laser can be easily concentrated onto a tiny point. It can thus produce enough heat to turn a metal, such as steel, into a vapor! Lasers can be used to make accurate cutting tools that can even cut through diamond, the hardest substance known.

Laser light and wavelength
White light from a flashlight can be thought of as a mixture of waves. Each wavelength represents a certain color. The waves making up a laser beam are quite different. Not only are all the waves the same length (color), but they are lined up so that the tops (peaks) of the waves coincide.

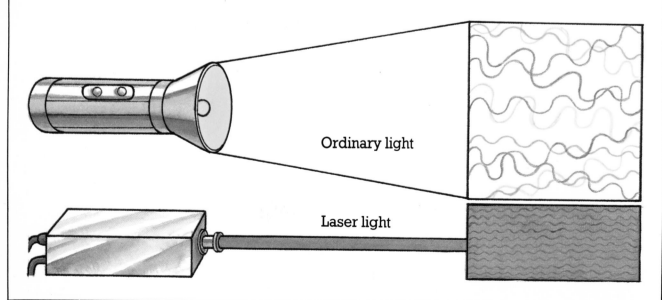

Ordinary light

Laser light

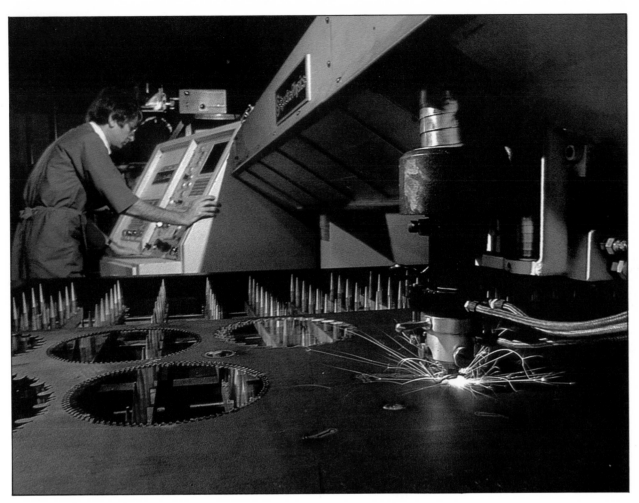

Beams of laser light are powerful enough to cut through metal

The various wavelengths making up white light can be separated by a prism. We know that laser light is all of one wavelength because it cannot be separated by a prism. Waves of laser light are all bent to the same extent by the prism since they all travel at the same speed through glass.

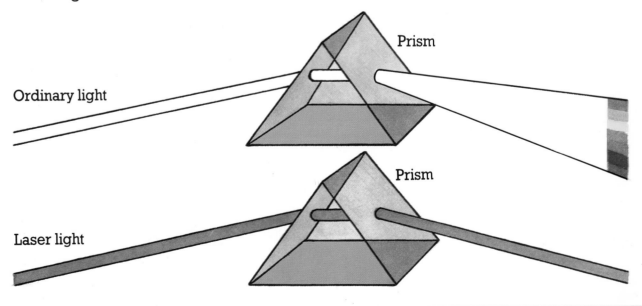

Prism

Ordinary light

Prism

Laser light

USE OF LASERS

Lasers are quickly becoming one of the most important developments of the century. There are many ways in which lasers can be used and more uses are still being discovered. The photographs show two areas in which lasers affect our lives. As well as making good cutting tools in industry, lasers make excellent "knives" for surgeons. The laser "knife" is completely sterile and seals small blood vessels as it cuts, so that less blood is lost. Laser light is often used to "weld" a retina, which has become detached, to the back of the eye. A detached retina is quite a common eye disorder.

Holograms are three-dimensional pictures made by illuminating objects with laser light. They look solid and real. Apart from being fascinating to look at, holograms are being used on credit cards as they are very difficult to forge.

The shiny appearance of a hologram produces a 3-D image

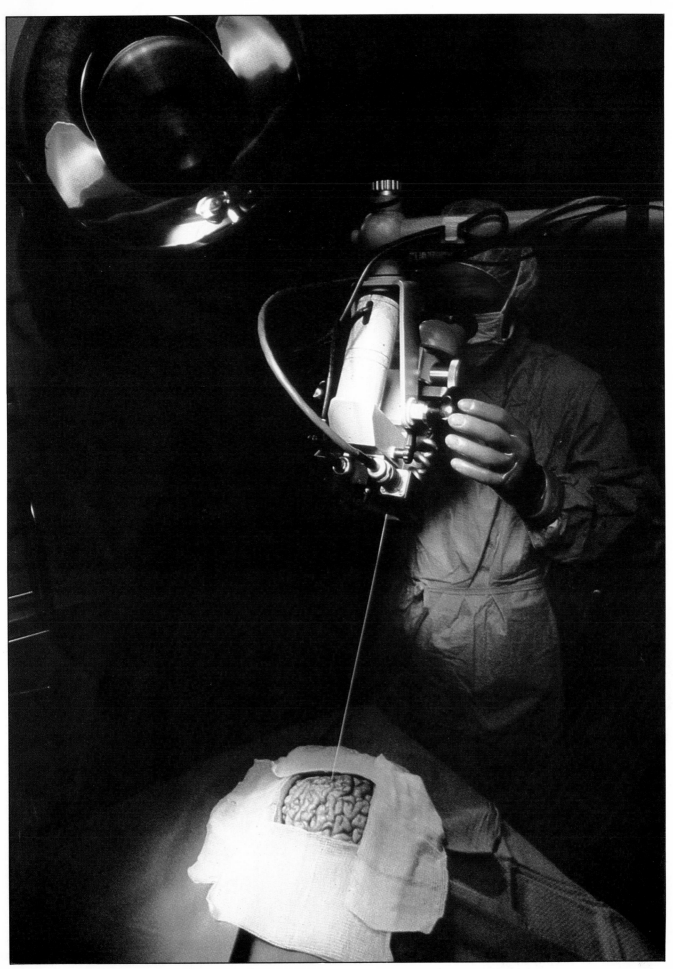

Lasers are often used in medicine, for example, in delicate brain surgery

MAKE YOUR OWN PERISCOPE

This periscope is made from a box containing two mirrors held at 45°. It can reflect light so that you can see over walls and around corners!

What you need

Two small mirrors (both the same size); some cardboard; a protractor for measuring the angles of the mirrors; a ruler; a pencil; scissors; adhesive tape; and a box of paints.

Measure the distances shown as A and B in the diagram. Make sure that the mirror is held at an angle of 45° while you do this (a protractor will help).

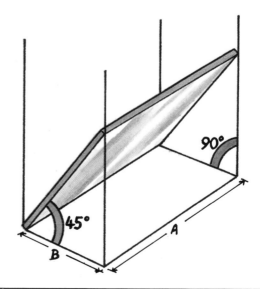

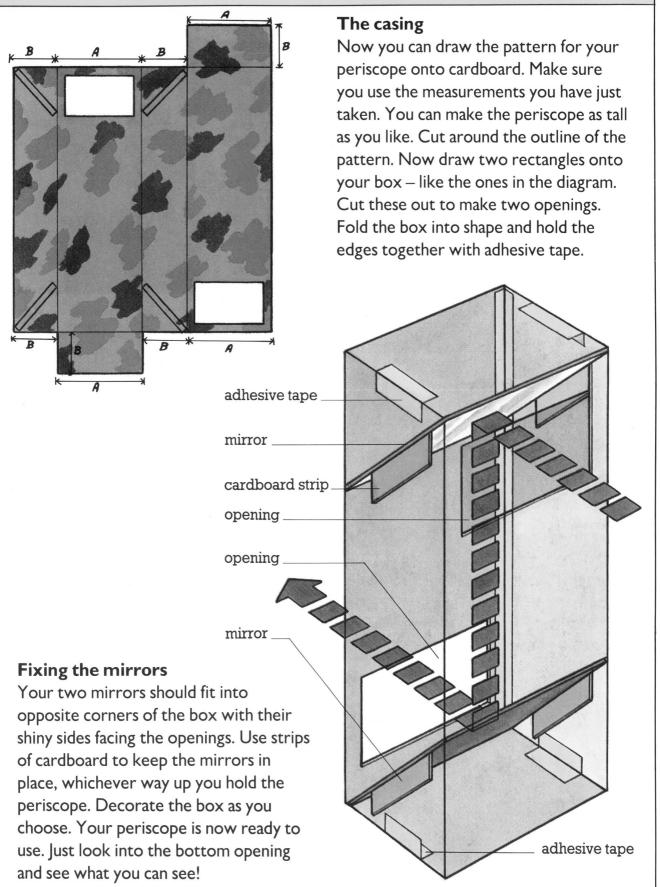

The casing

Now you can draw the pattern for your periscope onto cardboard. Make sure you use the measurements you have just taken. You can make the periscope as tall as you like. Cut around the outline of the pattern. Now draw two rectangles onto your box – like the ones in the diagram. Cut these out to make two openings. Fold the box into shape and hold the edges together with adhesive tape.

adhesive tape

mirror

cardboard strip

opening

opening

mirror

Fixing the mirrors

Your two mirrors should fit into opposite corners of the box with their shiny sides facing the openings. Use strips of cardboard to keep the mirrors in place, whichever way up you hold the periscope. Decorate the box as you choose. Your periscope is now ready to use. Just look into the bottom opening and see what you can see!

adhesive tape

Light waves

Light travels as waves – but what is a wave? You can make a wave by shaking one end of a ribbon. The up and down movement you make spreads along the length of the ribbon and appears as a wave. A wave is a way in which energy can move from one place to another. Light waves travel at an astonishing speed, faster than anything else we know of.

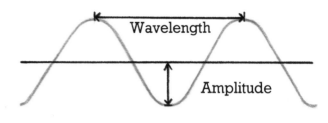

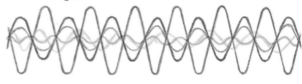

White light

The distance between the top of one wave and the next is known as the "wavelength." The depth of a wave is called its "amplitude." Each color of the spectrum has its own special wavelength and amplitude.

Measuring with light

Both large and small distances can be measured very accurately with laser light. In 1969 the Apollo 11 astronauts placed a mirror on the Moon. Scientists on Earth shined a laser beam toward the mirror and timed how long it took for the beam to be reflected back again. They knew the speed at which the light traveled and so they were able to work out the distance of the Moon from the Earth – to within just a few inches of the actual distance!

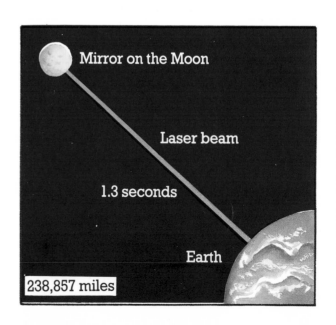

Mirror on the Moon

Laser beam

1.3 seconds

Earth

238,857 miles

GLOSSARY

Beam
A wide band of light going in a certain direction.

Binoculars
An instrument, fitted with convex lenses, for looking at distant objects – it makes them look closer.

Camera
An instrument that records images.

Darkness
The absence of light.

Focus
Adjust to make a clear image.

Image
The picture of an object that is produced by a lens or mirror.

Light
This is a type of wave that can be seen by the eye. It is also known as "visible light."

Microscope
An instrument that produces a large image of a very small object. It is used by biologists to observe small living things and their cells and tissues.

Nerve fibers
Fine threads of living tissue that carry messages to or from the brain or spinal cord. These messages are carried as electrical impulses.

Prism
A block of glass with triangular top and bottom and rectangular sides. It is used to refract light.

Pupil
The round hole at the front of the eye through which light passes. The size of the pupil alters according to the light.

Ray
A narrow band of light traveling in a certain direction.

Reflection
When light is bounced back off a surface, we say it is reflected. Everything reflects some light, but flat, polished or smooth surfaces are the best reflectors. Dull, uneven surfaces can only produce distorted reflections.

Refraction
When light passes from one material to another, its direction changes. We say that the light is being refracted. Refraction takes place because light travels faster through some substances than others.

Retina
The back of the eye. It is sensitive to light.

Telescope
An instrument for looking at distant objects. It is particularly useful for studying stars and planets.

INDEX

Photographic Credits:
Cover; Spectrum: contents page and pages 7, 17 and 21; Tony Stone: title page; Daily Telegraph: pages 6, 9 and 19; Zefa: page 11; Hutchinson: page 12; Picturepoint: page 15; GV Forrest: pages 22 and 27; Science Photo Library: pages 25 and 27; Art Directors.

PRINTED IN BELGIUM BY
INTERNATIONAL BOOK PRODUCTION